SEAN O'BRIEN'S twelve collections of poetry include *The Drowned Book* (2007), *Europa* (2018) and *Embark* (2022). His work has received awards including the T.S. Eliot Prize, the Forward Prize, and the E.M. Forster Award. His other work includes fiction, drama, criticism and translation. In 2020 his translation of the *Collected Poems* of the Kazakh national poet Abai Kunanbayuli was published, and in 2021 he edited Alistair Elliot's *This is the Life: Selected Poems*. His poems have been widely translated. He is Emeritus Professor of Creative Writing at Newcastle University and a Fellow of the Royal Society of Literature. He lives in Newcastle upon Tyne.

*Also by Sean O'Brien in Picador*

Embark

It Says Here

Europa

Collected Poems

The Beautiful Librarians

Once Again Assembled Here

November

Afterlife

The Drowned Book

The Firebox

Dante's Inferno

Cousin Coat

Downriver

*Sean O'Brien*

# The Bonfire Party

PICADOR POETRY

First published 2026 by Picador
an imprint of Pan Macmillan
The Smithson, 6 Briset Street, London EC1M 5NR
*EU representative:* Macmillan Publishers Ireland Ltd, 1st Floor,
The Liffey Trust Centre, 117–126 Sheriff Street Upper,
Dublin 1 D01 YC43
Associated companies throughout the world

ISBN 978-1-0350-6490-8

Copyright © Sean O'Brien 2026

The right of Sean O'Brien to be identified as the
author of this work has been asserted in accordance with
the Copyright, Designs and Patents Act 1988.

All rights reserved. No part of this publication may be reproduced,
stored in a retrieval system, or transmitted, in any form, or by any means
(including, without limitation, electronic, mechanical, photocopying, recording
or otherwise) without the prior written permission of the publisher.

Pan Macmillan does not have any control over, or any responsibility for,
any author or third-party websites (including, without limitation, URLs,
emails and QR codes) referred to in or on this book.

1 3 5 7 9 8 6 4 2

A CIP catalogue record for this book is available from the British Library.

Printed and bound in the UK using 100% Renewable Electricity by CPI Group (UK) Ltd

This book is sold subject to the condition that it shall not, by way of trade or otherwise,
be lent, hired out, or otherwise circulated without the publisher's prior consent in any form
of binding or cover other than that in which it is published and without a similar condition
including this condition being imposed on the subsequent purchaser. The publisher does not
authorize the use or reproduction of any part of this book in any manner for the purpose of
training artificial intelligence technologies or systems. The publisher expressly reserves
this book from the Text and Data Mining exception in accordance with Article 4(3)
of the European Union Digital Single Market Directive 2019/790.

Visit **www.picador.com** to read more about all our books and to buy them.

*For Bill Herbert*

# Contents

After Hölderlin   1

## 1.

Otherwise   5

Sleepers   6

Survivor   8

A Butcher   10

Bodies   12

Rites   13

Clearing   14

The Laurels   15

Peacetime   16

High Summer   17

Dead Man   19

The Courtyard   20

The Past   21

The Old Crowd   23

Of Sheds   24

Ryan: Rainy Season   25

Shelter 28

The Bonfire Party 29

## 2. Impasse: *for Jules Maigret*

Information Received 33

The Sacred Heart 34

Deluge 35

Chez Léon 36

Garagistes 37

Canal du Midi 39

Impasse 40

In the Zone 42

Oysters 43

Un Jeton 45

Skylight 46

Fin 48

## 3.

Terrain Vague 51

Blue Window 53

The Pool 54

The Afternoon in Question   56

Provincial Monsters   58

Hymn to Apollo   59

Bertran   60

Street of Clocks   61

The Prince of Aquitaine   63

Hello Stranger   64

Second Language   67

À la Carte   68

Siberian Birch   70

Desire   71

The Goodbye Look   72

To Cythera   74

Juniper   76

This is Not a River   77

Fingerpost   79

The Point   80


*Notes*   84

*Acknowledgements*   86

# After Hölderlin

Above all you must have by heart
the gaze of the roses, the heat of the sun,
the pool's green shade,
                        because blind and speechless
winter is coming, when the city's walls
will close and the weathercocks
clatter all day on the stormy roofs.
You have lived without history. No longer.

1.

# Otherwise

In the other life, when snow began to fall,
or more precisely when I noticed snow was falling
and that in the branches of the cherry tree
a blackbird had suspended nesting
not to tune his beak but look about him —

in that other life I might have known
how to encompass the event: snow falling
on the backs of houses, on stone walls and shed roofs,
on furniture abandoned in the lane
as if a localized catastrophe was barely over:

snow falling from a white sky whose resources
seemed unlimited, not settling yet,
not thick enough to count for anything —
and yet still snow as someone in the other life
might seek to represent it, a creation

waiting for a god and neither
ending nor beginning, only falling.

# Sleepers

*sleeping the deep, deep sleep of England,*
*from which I sometimes fear that we shall never wake*
*— George Orwell, Homage to Catalonia*

Our age of afternoons was ending
all that summer while we slept
the little sleep the English call their own.

Sleep was a pool the sun could never warm.
The surface lay unmoved
and sightless while the clouds swam on

across an empty screen into the past.
And that was it, a dim eternity.
Until the weather changed and there we were

again, dry-mouthed on burning beds,
half-listening as autumn thunderstorms
broke on the coast, and on the Downs

we didn't own (we had an understanding, though).
In any case, all this was surely meant
for somewhere else. This couldn't be the end

for something we had never thought to lose
because we had no names to call it by, because
we knew that language was a matter

best avoided: words were not the same
as everything we'd always known. That's why
we couldn't at that moment quite recall

whatever we were dying to forget,
and why we failed to recognize ourselves
when we were resurrected at the death

and pyres rose along the avenues
to meet the setting sun a minute sooner
every day, with summer never yet begun.

# Survivor

'Alles für Deutschland' — *a phrase illegal for its Nazi origins, reportedly used by Björn Höcke of AfD in a speech in 2021.*

His widow's spinster sisters planned
the death of Uncle Jack's piano,
the upright that he'd left at home —
not the one he would play in a lull
on the back of a lorry, the very same
Bedford three-tonner he rode into Belsen.

One day Jack came back from war
and went upstairs to smoke, to rest his eyes.
His instrument survived him, evidence
of people's palaces on dance-band nights,
and youth, when Jack could please himself
by pleasing others with a song.

And then it sat there, occupying space
with silence, patiently, like guilt.
*What is it really, Freda? Fancy clart. Get rid,*
and let the rag-and-bone man's axe expose
the smoky heaps of yellow teeth, piano-wire
and firewood for what they were.

*Freda, there'll never be room in a prefab.*
Somehow it escaped the massacre
to live in exile, secretly.
It holds its peace among the photographs
of his kids' grandkids born too late
to understand or even notice.

The dead will not be listening either.
Light up, Uncle Jack. Let's have a tune.
Let's roll out the barrel and hang out
the washing from the Siegfried Line
to the oven's mouth, where there is no one
left to care if smoke gets in your eyes.

# A Butcher

The butcher in his small black car drives out
through the gates of his secretive yard
in a slum at the back of the slums, a Hull corner
missed by the bombs, where the poor make do.
His head is the head of a horse, all teeth
and frantic eyes, his hair a grey bog-brush,
the immense hands pink and priestly
at the wheel, a Woodbine for a thurible.
On the back seat, sides of meat are sitting up
on blood-soaked newsprint. He'll be fined.

At the end of the day, he drives the car
back through the gates, and nobody knows
what happens in there afterwards, except
they can all hear a clopping, like hooves,
and when it stops, and when the music starts.
The kids playing out in the street can tell
that all of this, whatever this can be,
and come to that the whole of everything,
is 'from the war', a kind of sick-note
everyone must carry at all times and forever –

the butcher, the policeman, the priest,
the Jewish baker Mr Dietch, and Mrs Dietch,
and the Irish lady doctor Dr Buckley,
chain-smoking in her surgery and saving us
from polio and diphtheria. At sunset
the windows catch fire. Children are starving
in Europe. We should count our blessings,
sausage by sausage, chop by chop. Give thanks
to the butcher, whose gross pink meticulous hands
are always cold, the brothers of his meat.

# Bodies

The mirror on the mantelpiece lost interest
long ago. It finds it hard to concentrate
when I show up a lifetime afterwards
to see these strangers lying where they fell,
on tangled sheets in freezing student flats
that smell of smoke. There's nothing burning now
and even vanity's long since cast off
the outworn party-dresses, earrings, pillowed hair,
the smudged mascara on the faces
life could never show me in this grave and regal state.

While time absents itself, it leaves a shade
to mark its passage here: the tired white
of bodies left behind in tall distempered rooms
like sanatoria whose patients are the dead.
But here inside this dim late afternoon
that none of us have ever left, they are awake.
They watch me watching. It appears
that since there's nowhere else to be
and no time like the present, we must share
the fear and sweat and nakedness once more.

# Rites

Just as the grave of a sailor floods
when he exhales, just as the airman's plot
is marked by flaming barrels in a field,

just as the soldier lies where he fell
with his helmet placed at a rakish slant
on the butt of his rifle, just as the butcher

is flayed and the baker cremated,
just so the candlestick-maker has not
been spotted for quite some time.

# Clearing

*Nay, give me eyes, and light, lest that I sleep in dying.*
  — Psalm 13, translated by Sir Philip Sidney

Felled trunks in loden greatcoats lie
on the edge of a clearing: officers,
disarmed, beheaded, awaiting disposal.

Wreathed in the smoke of his creation,
pipe in hand, a hatchet for an axiom,
a Master comes this way once more.

When I am done, he says, the sound
of this wind in this wood is true silence
because it is mine and the world is over.

Yet here you are, still wandering waist-deep
in rusty ferns and amputated limbs.
What else can I tell you? Death's work

goes on, in a different part of the wood.
Nodding and smoking, he makes to leave.
What is a man if not his work? he asks.

What better work than this, the duty
in which death and benediction meet
and all this brash begins to burn?

# The Laurels

In this grey-green heaven of the north
the rain itself is so discreet that you can glimpse it
only in the mirrors in this ample grey stone house
whose arrow-slits you have no reason to approach.
Here all the rain that ever fell
is kept like property, in cisterns far below
these laurel bushes in their Barbour camouflage.

What is your business here? Look to your manners.
This is where money lies dreaming,
the grey vault where heaven is buried.
Whether no one ever lived here, whether everyone is dead,
this is an outcome, a sufficiency, a moiety
from slaves and sugar, hardwood and spices.
All that never happened happened here

in the House of Shaws by Rennie Mackintosh,
cold as the burnt-out core of the earth
suspended in its lead-lined afterlife. And the dead
do not believe in you, and they receive no visitors.
The house is closed, its faithful keepers put to sleep
and standing guard with one eye open
in the dark. Be sure you have no business here.

# Peacetime

Under the sunlit vault of the station
time too is waiting, with the Temperance Seven
and Flanders and Swann and a tiny young woman
escorted by a double bass in funeral black.
Whatever is possible glints in the distance
where tracks curve away under bridges
and over the soupy, slow-gliding Ouse, beyond York
to the land where the North is in earnest.
Slowly the Pennines rouse themselves to travel on
and Ocean spreads his cloak of royal blue
on the stony shore of Thornwick Bay, killing time
for sunstruck trippers who stand there for hours
with one foot in the water, staring at a smudge of smoke
that is sailing away and away but is never quite gone,
bearing a richly ambiguous cargo of uncles
stiff with concertinas and doubloons, away
to the pink edge of empire that bleeds from the map
like a water-painting book reversed by magic.
Oh, it could be worse. It will be worse. But while time waits,
the books displayed on barrows all along the pier
are fluttering open like applause remembering
against the odds, the words undaunted, saying quietly
to those with ears to hear that this time, while it lasts
*there's no discouragement / shall make us once relent.*

# High Summer

*for G*

Any day now, the leaves that almost touch
across the single lane will glow
brass-edged, but not quite yet:

high summer on an unadopted road
between two places history is done with.
Your dead are buried here: quarrymen, carters,

soldiers and maids-of-all-work. Imagine
they've been waiting out the centuries
to sense the wry, embarrassed tenderness

a visitor bestows upon the earth
while walking at a loss among the stones
where nowadays the odd parishioner

keeps down the grass as once his sisters
changed the flowers at St Chad's or St Peter
ad Vincula whose wealth is shadows.

This used to be England
and now it is nowhere. The map
can hardly wait to take its leave

for all the dead in dutiful array
have kept their patience and their place,
each summer and each bone-frost as it comes.

What happened. What will happen.
What the breeze that comes and goes
among the holm-oaks and the ash-trees stirs

but the place cannot utter, concerning
high summer, the presence of nowhere,
love and death consorting as they must.

# Dead Man

The dead man waking in the hedgerow,
bound in last year's ivy, lies and listens –
seagulls, trains, the vault of heaven. He apprehends
the scraping of a cleaner's bucket
on a flagstone in the nave as carefully
as Bonaparte's artillery, the ocean or a voice
in an attic crying no no no. The earth turns over.

He lies and listens to the slow upwelling
of the mosses in the merest hinted fissure
in the path beside the back door of the garage,
which will open any moment with a gasp of rust,
releasing oily ancient air and warmth
where spiders have been working double shifts
to swag the rafters and the window frames.

Here is a place prepared. It begins. It is good
on the whole. The dead man turns to sleep once more
with one ear open for a drop of rain
new-born a mile above, beginning its descent
into perfection, sent to shake the ruff
of the preoccupied narcissus, and for a moment
raise its empty face from self-regard.

# The Courtyard

The disposition of the shadows
alters with each glance. You asked for this,
the time to read, to pause and stare
down into the courtyard while an afternoon
unwrites itself. A chapter, then another.

Now the eastern wall is half-submerged
in shade. Up to its neck there, leaning
in a parody of sleep, a bicycle awaits
instructions. This is how the old ones lived
before the clocks conspired to agree.

A girl, her grave long since forgotten,
might appear beyond the gateway
with a bucket that a horse you never see
will drink from as the cities of the plain
go up in smoke, when for want of a nail

the kingdom is lost and the face of the waters
is darkened. Now read on, and weep
for the eternity in which that girl
who never was is almost here, still braced
against the bucket's dripping weight.

# The Past

The past was never waiting for us then.
Nor is it waiting for us now. It doesn't need us
to improve it, or fulfil it, set it right
or visit on it the peculiar love
with which we long to see ourselves
inside it once again, though we were never there
but merely present, both too early and too late.
I think of you, Miss Rook, and my friend Stephen Soldin.

An afternoon of drawing with crayons
on blue sugar-paper: the subject, war, as always.
I think especially of Stephen Soldin,
how ten years on we slipped behind the hoardings
in the persons of Labiche and Papa Boule
to scramble up the clinkered slope beside
the railway bridge on Perth Street West
when steam was dying but not dead.

We'd place a penny on the rail and crouch there
waiting for the gust of ash to swallow us and go.
After Suez, after rationing, words we knew
but didn't understand, the world had ended.
Yet there seemed to be a war for us to wage
in secret round the backs of hedges, bridges, sidings
and the Woolsheds' eerie miles of asphalt
stretching into scrub and oozy ponds and rumour.

In Miss Rook's class we'd always known
it was our duty to depict the European theatre
and the war at sea, Miss Rook patrolling
while we worked, so out in my Atlantic
fleets engaged and overturned and sank
beneath the coarse blue swell, with waves of fighters
plunging from the sun to rain down shells
on what was not already blazing. One day

I decided part of heaven should be blank.
This act could not escape Miss Rook's attention.
'What's that?' 'I don't know, Miss.' 'Well, fill it in.
We'll have no more of that now. Understand?'
But that was never true, just as the past had never
ended or begun but went on never being there,
like Judith Bolch and Maureen Donovan and Sharon Spandler
and the rest. It holds no trace of them: why should it?

I'm right, you know, Miss Rook, while you yourself
are less than dust, with all the other rooks.
I've no idea what Stephen Soldin makes of this.
But looking back to Perth Street Bridge
in silence, through some steam-obsessive's photograph,
I can confirm, examining the iron arch
that frames the bleached-out space beyond,
that nothing will be passing over it or underneath,

nor ever did, nor ever did. I shouldn't wait.

# The Old Crowd

The old crowd, what became of them,
possessors of that table in the window?
Week in, week out, they seemed both stunned
and glad to find each other still alive
to buy a round, or in one case begrudge it.
God knows what they found to talk about.

They liked to see the girls go by from work,
then as the evening deepened pass again, adorned
like goddesses, back-combed and insolent
and all too late. The old crowd knew their place.
Don't say a word. Quick now. The table's free.
Good evening, ladies. Do ignore us. Thank you.

# Of Sheds

*'they keep us from our Schlosses'*


Every shed is terrible, the tomb
of the inconsequent and furtive,
stuffed with secrets not worth keeping,
bradawls, buckets, mounds of bugger-all,
plus countless yellow catalogues of same –

Eldorado banal of the gadgie,
wonky shrine to Lollobrigida,
smelling of oil and ancient sweat and swarf
and something underneath all that
too vile to qualify for language.

Location, wise men say,
is everything. This place? This shed? By definition
this is nowhere. Gina fades
and no birds sing. The kettle's on. Come in.

# Ryan: Rainy Season

My kind lack the background when the rain is real
like this, when the rain comes seeking not
our inconvenience but our extinction.

These gingery days when the leaves come down
at last, and heavy-lidded manholes weep
for Bazalgette and all his works,

the rain is creaturely and pitiless
and sudden, in a range of formats.
This should be our tragedy, a time to act

with pure irrational righteousness,
to put off politesse and do some smiting.
Baseball bats and razors, fine, but fauna better –

yet which of us along these sinking streets
could access insect larvae for insertion
in her lover's ear, emerging only when

they've laid their eggs to drive the bastard mad –
as fanciful as Fortunato waking
in his bricked-up tomb, and yet for some

the boredom of the teenage years insists,
and they find themselves back in the attic
searching for the crate of special stuff

to read again beneath the streaming skylight
deep into the afternoon. From that concealed
curriculum we learned that sex is death

and the reverse is true, up to a point.
For this engorged enlightenment, bestowed
by all those sweating pages, we must thank

Van Thal among the connoisseurs of cruelty
and evil. How could politics compete? How could
the drowning world? Or love? Or anything?

Read your evil nonsense, yellow page
on page so mouldered now the thumb
with which you hold it flat will pass right through.

The mind is stupefied by rain and evil,
confined to one locality. Sewage comes
slithering out of the manhole and over the step

to meet itself emerging from the cellar
and then take the stairs at a lick. Now
what can you hear from inside the rain

in your chambers of rot? Tales like these
with their whispering filth. Be not afraid,
since history's a reservoir of corpses.

If we were really men, true gin-sunk
Haileybury washouts, rubber-planting stoics,
chaps the snakes are always watching,

we would need no telling. We would know
the world is only ever scenery, a tale,
and this last inundation, this surrender

to the overbrimming glass of gin and bitters,
to the flood, and to the seething residents
within the deepest passage of the ear

who blindly tunnel to the brain itself —
all this is fate, a sick nobility conferred
upon the undeserving as a gift,

as mould emerges from a wall, the spawn
of time and damp, digesting its estate.

# Shelter

Under a dripping arch of the railway,
this is the weather-god seeking shelter
with a torn cagoule, amnesia for company
and absent-minded lightning
jumping from his hair and finger-ends.

Beyond saving, they say, sleeping rough
on the cobbles, in that pool
of fretful electricity, son of Don't Care,
here to illustrate the moral.
Boil him, fry him, still he Don't.

The weather-god had everything
but irony, and if the mind of the divinity
is literal, it comes to this, the death
from which they had to make him first
and then forget, as he forgets.

Oh now stand clear, they say.
Stand clear of what? Stand where?

# The Bonfire Party

*5th November 1933*

Ravilious would prefer the fireworks autumn-brown,
but something must be seen to shed some light
on this imaginary English town
on this imaginary Bonfire Night
between the wars, between the funeral games.

See those ecstatic dancers wearing horses' heads,
and Vulcan in his good grey suit, who feeds the flames
and doesn't hear whatever she's just said,
that woman with her raised admonitory hands.
Her sisters stand on guard to feed the blaze

with branches, but he doesn't understand,
possessed by immolation, while the neighbours gaze
across the wall, a pair who seem much older,
burdened with sobriety but ready to fulfil
the duties of the tolerant beholder

whose achievement lies in simply standing still.
A boy in shorts and men who should know better
sprint past the open pub towards a hidden square
but since it's art, the spirit not the letter,
let us suppose there's really something there,

a crossroads at the centre of the night
where anything may be if we possess our souls
in patience, watch the crowd run out of sight,
and let these pediments and architraves console
our ignorance with what we think we feel.

White steps walk up into the dark, past windows
brighter than the sun, towards a Catherine wheel
that ought to light the way to Dante's *Paradiso*.
This town must be Italy. It must be Eastbourne.
It's a feast-day feud. It's Guelphs v. Ghibellines.

The soundless detonations boast and warn
but no one's here to tell us what it means.
Up on the roofs, where watchers climb
from skylights to enjoy the larger view
intended for the many not the few,

can what they see be nothing less than time
at work to salt the heavens with new stars
that weep themselves away and fall to earth,
like Aphrodite who was present at the birth
of Lucifer and all his avatars?

# 2.

## IMPASSE
for Jules Maigret

# Information Received

The concierge. The slaughterman. The pharmacist.
The bargee. The cabaret dancer. Twist.
The dealer in antiquities. The con. The one
with no visible means of support
and a passage booked from an unknown port.
The Belgian or the Latvian. Lorraine. Alsace.
Oh all the perfumes of Arabia and Grasse.
The negligée, the nun and the informer.
On nights like these, says Lucas, *nessun dorma*.
The *condamné à mort*, the cadaver, the tout.
The iron certainty that while the truth will out –
sing up, my friends, we are the policemen's choir –
the facts alone cannot explain desire.

# The Sacred Heart

Behind the hidden towns
that coal has long abandoned,
barges full of ash still ply
the old canals, still hauled
by the skeletons of horses.
You find the locks almost intact,
the rusted gear still turning,
cottages half in the woods
suspicious still, their gaze
averted and omniscient.
Someone should corroborate
these facts, but everyone
is either sleeping or deceased.
Instead there is a room,
all corners, with a yellow smell
of want and poor digestion,
plus a glass of glaring teeth
beside the Sacred Heart,
and all of this belongs to France,
the heart of yellow-grey
long dead and beating still.

# Deluge

Long before you feel it, you can hear prolonged applause
as from a concert hall across a square, intensifying steadily,
then in a moment everywhere. It is not the épuration,
only rain, which everyone has always known,
to which there can be no exceptions, rain
known also as desire, manifest in sudden pools
and urgent gutters, in the silver-pewter gleam of cobblestones,
in the sealed-off courtyards of the rich, and in the Seine itself
that for the moment lies accepting what must be.
Although the heart longs at such times to be cleansed
of its sins of omission and lust and all the occasions of sin,
life must go on. The murderer shaking the rain from his hat
ascends by elevator to his crime. A dancer must bathe
in the backstage sink and bicker with the pianist over money.
She was offered Monte Carlo once, remember. New York.
She dresses, puts on kohl and leaves as if she has decided
once and for all, tossing the curls that helped to bring her to this pass.
It is desire, when the clock beside the bed is close to death from waiting
and the rain is beating on the fanlight. You will never see it all – the city
with its million needs and sorrows, but you know at least
that happiness is relative: to sit at home and read the paper
while Madame is sewing and the radio brings news
of further executions is enough. It must be. Or what else?

# Chez Léon

Depopulated entrepôt, declining since Napoleon,
to be renounced in due course by the sea.

Locks and bridges go on opening
before the dawn, marine automata

inured to life as mud and brine
interpret it, while nothing berths or sails.

No sooner in the town than out.
Long dunes. The dark flats going nowhere

past the bar, Chez Léon, whose patron stands
transfixed at the tin counter-top

by his own dark face above it
in the mirror with the bottles,

staring back, as irredeemable as coinage
from a failed republic, weighing in the palm

he has extended to his shadow-self
the payment for the passage he is owed.

# Garagistes

*Nothing special. A reliable Dugat 12 with a boot
big enough to stuff a couple of corpses in, if necessary.*
— Nestor Burma


In this paradise of *garagistes*, everything is far away.
It will be night. It will be raining. So the world
is not accessible from here, my friends.
Only killers and detectives are abroad,
apart, that is, from lovers' corpses
sprawling in the ditches, with their pitiable candour
anguished in the fleeting moonlight.
In flooded fields the harrows rust and groan
at their condition: one might think a war
was fought on this terrain, among the cabbage-stalks
and superannuated implements. Not so,
though this *Département* and the 'nerveless crooks'
who claim to farm it are possessive of their share
of abject national misery. The bicycles of priests
must plough a lonely furrow here: the pathos
of the cleric is to have no information any more.
I share his ignorance and his despair.
I understand and sometimes I forgive,
but this remains the paradise of *garagistes*
where petrol and not grace is of the essence –
no petrol: no death: no Panhard: no murder –
and of legendary rarity, its only source
these moon-faced men in blue, disguised

as petrol pumps, the self-same *garagistes*
whose wives could well be next to die
for gazing at the *camionneurs*. You understand.
So then, where is your murder? Show me. Tell me.
Now bring torches. Call the distant capital
for men who can be trusted in this dark, like Janvier.
There is no telephone, you say. So then.
Bring me the girl and the indigent driver.
I will question them. No? Are they sleeping?
In the stable? Wake them. Wake them.
Are they dead? Then wake them anyway!

# Canal du Midi

Still as ever, the Canal du Midi
keeps its counsel, beckoning us on
beneath the curving arch of willows.
We know the world is somewhere else,
but it is hard to say what leaves us
disinclined to linger when we hear
the summer boats approach once more
like a cortège, with due solemnity,
as if they were the past, weighed down
with businessmen and their unsmiling girls.

No record has been found of the noyade
of the local SS officer commanding
or the Milice *chef de groupe* with whom
it is alleged he had been speaking
when the door burst open. Everything
is academic after that. The waters close
over the murderers' heads at last.
Three streets of quince-coloured stone
continue waiting as before. The sun
goes inching past. That is not evidence.

# Impasse

There is an unexpected halt at the frontier
between these pages and a *roman dur*.
Rain, darkness, the despair of rational *horlogerie*.
In Paris, Janvier and Lucas wait
suspended with a beer in one hand
and a sandwich in the other, needing orders.
From the corridor you see a field of dirty snow
beyond the platform where the stationmaster waits,
examining his fob-watch, wincing
as if time is shouting reprimands
from far away but not quite far enough.
A woman stirs a bitter pan of soup and adds
her pinch of disappointment: you know this
though you cannot see it, just as you infer
a drunken bicycle approaching slowly
on the bank of a canal. There follows
an exasperated huff of steam, and next
the brutal crash and ring of couplings.
Nonetheless the train is quite unmoved
and goes on creaking to itself in private.
In this moment it is clear a death
will be required if the journey's to continue.
But to kill someone is hard; to kill her
in the tiny lavatory along the corridor,
obstructed by the sink, with both the parties
slipping on a floor awash with water —
difficult, and time-consuming too.

Yet since this evening you are neither here nor there
you will not intervene. Possess your soul
in patience and go back to the compartment,
where the jacket of your book says Flaubert,
and a look inside will show your preference
for *série noir* to while the time away.

# In the Zone

Last week is a long time ago.
A year? Ten years? Beyond imagining.
The people you are thinking of are dead.
Not even the sulphurous waters
could save them from diseases
of the liver, or lachrimae rerum.
This sleeping town is where they live
in their retirement, modestly.
Laval was shot, the Marshal spared.
Now lunchtime is upon us
and the owner of the bookshop
locks his door and disappears.
There will be no developments.
The same few pensioned wraiths
complete a turn around the gardens
and approach their chosen tables
as the waiter rises from the grave
to greet his patrons. Nothing
can be told or altered now.
These are the dead, and yet they live,
and they remember nothing
and say less. I ask you, who is pure?
And how much room does evil occupy?

# Oysters

*Sensible, commonplace, beyond understanding*
                     – Douglas Dunn, 'The Clear Day'

When you lay sleepless on the train, you longed
as a faraway convict might long, for the cold
white wine of this region, where the final glass
holds a few grains of sand. But this one is sour.
That night you hoped for oysters too –
but it's neap tide, when none can be gathered:
clinging to their sunken stakes they wait
for death, unblinking in the salty dark.
And you're a spy from Paris, here to stick your nose
in matters which are none of your concern.

The corpse arrives by cart. The women
flood the little church, and in the square
their men are busy drinking. The deceased
was loathed by one and all but must be
honoured nonetheless as one of theirs,
the postmistress who opened all the mail
and eavesdropped on their dreams,
a dismal reptile known to be immortal
until someone chopped her into bits.
They see her buried, just in case.

But you they will not give the time of day.
Liars and murderers, every last one.
There's nothing to be done about it now.
And when they've watched you board the train
to Poitiers and, for all they care, perdition,
they will broach an oyster-barrel and uncork
the icy wine, and watch their sun go down
in the companionable silence of a truce,
in this their ménage of heaven and hell —
*sensible, commonplace, beyond understanding.*

# Un Jeton

Replenishing the barrel of the body
with *une pression*, you call the patron back:
you need a *jeton* for the telephone,
that oracle of murder. This time when you call
perhaps the girl you said you'd ring, the girl
you promised you'd keep safe, is gone.
You keep the token in your hand. Best wait for luck,
you think. If someone has to die –
although you wish for no one's death –
it would be fairer if the jealous older man
was dealt the ace of spades for once, and she
did not lie bleeding in the bath.
You drink. You smoke. You wait and see,
and idly stroke the face of Marianne.

# Skylight

When you open the skylight you stand waist-deep
in the roof. It is icy and clear. The beauty of it:
to arrive in the *arrondissement* of sky and chimneys
at the far end of the night, where nothing more
can be required of you. The evildoers
have escaped; the good are sleeping.
Then, as it grows light, the radios
on all the floors on all the avenues
crank up their broken hearts. *Que reste-t-il
de nos amours?* Innumerable unknown
others take their places at the windows.
You have reason to suspect that still
they wonder why the world can be no different.
They read their fortunes in the rainy glass –
a scatter of diminishing acquaintance,
unobtainable advancement, pain
that might be love but does not speak
the language of itself, and after that
God knows how many chill provincial towns,
each with its unique demented patience
waiting to consume these failures,
these ungrateful children when at last
they lapse from disaffection to indifference
and come home to learn what they deserve.
You feel the chill and stir yourself. The bells
are scattering the pigeons. Satanists
dismantle their equipment and depart

from rooms that smell of sweat and incense.
An empty metro goes past, full of longing.
Yes, you are still here. You leave a cloud of breath
like someone in the distance drawn by Tardi.
Now the trail is cold. If you could lay
your hands on life you would have done so
long ago. You close the skylight
carefully, beginning the descent.

# Fin

The day when crime shall be no more,
when desire and loss are spent like lovers
and want of motive cancels opportunity
and candlesticks are unambiguously
candlesticks and in the wardrobes
there are only suits and dresses
queuing patiently in scented darkness –

the day when crime shall be no more
will find you in your braces, waiting, smoking,
looking out on to the evening *quai*.
So where are Janvier and Lucas now?
The telephone has ceased to ring.
You pick up the receiver. Listen. Nothing.
You will not believe a word of it.

3.

# Terrain Vague

*for Gilles Ortlieb*

Abandoned allotments gone over to brambles,
unbuilt on since there is no road.

Stone gateposts of a house the kids demolished
at their leisure, where the smell of smoke

still lingers decades afterwards.
A nowhere such as this attracts

the walker on a dimming winter afternoon
without an end in view. It seems

to be a summing-up, to pass the hour
here instead of somewhere else. Meanwhile

the head is emptying of everything except
the sound of trains so far off now

they must be memory, the disenchanted
spell of cities seeming to forget themselves

in absent spaces, terrains vagues manqués,
the victory of nothing taking place.

It might be happiness. It might
exact no name, yet here you are

still turning up as though for work
among these marginalia – the brambles'

ever-breaking wave, the zing of running feet
beneath the bridge, the eye

insatiable and used to making do
with what is left, the frosty moon,

the almost-silence, like an indrawn breath,
between two trains.

# Blue Window

*the horror of aesthetics*
– Douglas Dunn

Blue window pouring down into the room
to ride this surf of smoking light
until it breaks against the furniture

and round our ankles. I can quite believe it.
Nothing is impossible, as witness me
about to edit Ugolino's table-talk,

complete with tasting notes. Best eaten cold.
Or there's that group of scrunty hawthorns
stooping at the ditch-line in the blast

across the Durham steppe, their gaze
averted from the train – like peasants
spying mounted Florentines, like nymphs

turned crones to duck the god's attention.
All the while, the waterfall of light
continues in the house beside the sea,

until the windows are inseparable from water
and the breaking wave's a blessing
nothing warrants, breaking none the less.

# The Pool

*I thought I saw a wolf*
                        – Randall Jarrell

Bulrushes, a lifebelt, birches leaning in
to catch their reflections, shedding leaves
the colour of October on the water
where princesses come to drown. There's more:
the pool's a scrying-glass the rain falls through
into the other forest and the other pool below.
If you consult this mirror three times over
neither half is certain of its whereabouts
and you have changed an accident
into a narrative, like the naïf sent out
to gather firewood, who is beguiled
though well aware he should not linger here.
When you began, today was surely August,
but falling leaves and sentry-coughs
reveal a company of rooks in winter quarters,
crouching in their sodden cloaks to write
their memoirs of the Grande Armée
with quills plucked from themselves,
in inky blood, in disenchantment:
Wagram, Eylau in the snowstorm,
and then the broken starving army dancing
on the ice, and under it, at Berezina.
What have these to do with fairy-tales –
except, look now, an underwater ballroom

swagged in weedy crimson, full of cloudy mirrors,
sees a host of butchered gentlemen
revolving with princesses in their arms.
And what has that to do with this dim pool
you found by chance, and looked in for too long,
and how will you get home from here,
unless this is the only world
and you are home already? Soldier
from the wars returning, set your burden down,
arrange these twigs, take out your tinder-box,
and make a fire if you can, by which to read
this tale of maidens, beasts and bloodshed
dreamed by history, to pass the time away.

# The Afternoon in Question

A storm of photons lends the sky its blue,
while the corona may be fiercer than the heart
of this, 'our minor star'. How fond we seem to be
of denigration, when a fact discovered in a book
may be dismissed on that account alone.
The solitude of afternoons
is altogether harder to despise,
since we are implicated in their emptiness,
no matter we have never been equipped or trained
to meet the vast demands the frozen hours make,
or see beyond the blue light out of which descends
this sense of loss that gains our cowed consent
by promising us nothing in return.
But afternoon remains to navigate
between these hoarded papers and the great outdoors,
which at the least encouragement unpacks its samples,
showing rooks in line astern along the roof,
and hawthorns waving witches' knickers, ragged
from a winter in the wind, redundant chimneys'
blackened hoods – all these as brisk and definite
as the inspection copies I was given 'to peruse'
while waiting in my mother's office at her school.
By five o'clock the playground found its silence,
the corridors were sleeping, and a smell of pencils
leaked beneath the stockroom door like Christmas
and austerity. The Three Unlucky Men
went to their doom, and when the smugglers rode by

I turned to face the wall. I overheard
a quarrel on the saltmarsh and another silence
falling from a clear blue sky, the day
the Piper sealed the hill behind the children.

# Provincial Monsters

Dear provincial monsters
oozing from their mausolea,
up the stairs and through the keyhole,
pausing to reconstitute
before they do the business —
where would we be without them?
Who would terrorize the fen?
Extirpate them? Burn the records?
What then, I ask, what then?

# Hymn to Apollo

On Fenkle Street at dusk the god approaches.
Or the god departs from Cowen's monument.

The god is anyway in motion: his gliding walk
with the bulb of fennel raised aloft

to light the way in green. The god
breaches the door of the Grammar School

which seals itself behind him. The god
is next seen (by drunks or a vacant 'creative'

staring down from a bathroom window)
to be crossing the moat, selecting a tribute

in fruit from the Priory garden, then
veering towards Gallowgate, the Milburn Stand

and Leazes Park, whose lake is frozen
where the god strides effortlessly on

to Spittal Tongues and every other place
that needs his brand of medicine,

the gift, the opportunity, the curse
green-tongued and bitter at the root.

# Bertran

See how the lamp is worn under the arm
or carried aloft as a head —
too late for salvation, too late perhaps
even to warn, but stylish
nonetheless, according to its lights.

# Street of Clocks

A message came. The message said:
*Go to the Street of Clocks. Today.*
But it was early, so I strolled
along the Street of Knives
because I meant to go equipped.
And having sourced my blade,
I pawned my ring somewhere
along the Impasse of the Silversmiths,
and with the money bought
a pie, along the Street of Pies.
This I consumed at leisure
in the gardens by the zoo
while looking at the thousand girls
who passed me by. Then glancing up
I saw that the cathedral clocks
all indicated noon was gone.
But they were always wrong –
and yet the streets had emptied
in a moment, so at last
I passed into the Street of Love
and climbed the endless stairs
to reach the attic where you waited,
so I thought, but there I found
no sign of you except a pair of
turquoise earrings on the mantelpiece.
Then lateness came upon me
suddenly, and down I went

to seek the Street of Clocks,
to do as I had been instructed –
long ago, it seemed by then –
and after that, who knows? I thought
I'd heard of it, this Street of Clocks,
but till that day had never visited
the far-off quarter where it stood.
So on I went, and time went by,
under the railway and over the river,
and if there was a Street of Clocks –
and who, I ask you, would
invent one? – no, I never found it,
though I walked and walked
until my feet were bare,
under the railway and over the river,
till midnight came and I was done.

*translated from the Polish of Kazimierz Borka (1888–1937)*

# The Prince of Aquitaine

*after Nerval*

I am a shadow, the widower, the inconsolable,
the Prince of Aquitaine in his demolished tower.
My star is dead, my starry lute inlaid
with the black sun of melancholia.

In this entombing night, give me again
that comfort you once offered me: Tyrrhenian
Posillipo whose winding columbine
could ease my heart among the vines and roses.

Am I love? Am I Apollo? Lusignan or Berowne?
My brow still blushes from the kisses of the Queen.
I've dreamed among the sea-caves with the Siren . . .

And I alone have forded Acheron both ways,
with my cithara tempered equally to serve
the cries of sibyls and the saints in ecstasy.

## Hello Stranger

*Où sont nos amis morts?*
— Baudelaire, *Intimate Journals*

You say in Paris you'd have been allowed
to usher your lobster aboard, just in time
for the annunciation of modernity
by means of disaster: with infinite scruple
and slow as a planet, the train falls
head-first off the Gare Montparnasse.

Yet here you are, minus lobster and luggage,
alone on a bench in the cold in Pearson Park
between the council's hooded roses and the Queen
on her cast iron plinth. She gives no sign,
but cannot like the look of you, Mr Ambassador,
eyeing the interview outfit — pyjamas

plagiarized from Robert Lowell on the grounds
that he would never miss them, being mad.
So where are your fur and the ruby ring,
or your sinister friends who wore the same get-up
but learned on the job as you never quite could
how to fashion themselves for the times?

Among the hunters in the snow you are the one
who's left his boots behind, but this is this.
And your mission today? Wait here for the present,
still rolling your own from a sacred box
in case you find a cure for emphysema,
still talking of poetry, of Faustus, talking

of your many wives, 'a number not yet ascertained',
putting in a bid for fifty quid or the price of a shave
or 'two old pennies to cover my eyes'. Even now
I hope for your reform, the 'proper job', although
you found 'to be a proper man quite awful'.
Caught between devil and thalassopelagic

you took to drugs like a brick to water.
Snow falls out of the sun. In the deserted park
the linden avenues march off towards the gates.
The moon has paused and this is neither
dusk nor dawn, and that's enough cosmology.
Remember, Faustus, thou art damned,

and on the furnace-plains of hell must hold converse
with sundry boring monomaniacs. Damned
to forever beginning again, to unearthing
the failure concealed in the next piece of luck,
to drying out and dying *und so weiter, und so weiter*,
in venues from the Düsserl to the Humber,

to making the case for delirium tremens.
One eyebrow rises when you mean to speak,
and with the shy Hitlerian moustache
you look like a matinée idol who's fallen
face-first on to concrete over and over.
But setting that aside, you say, all this —

as you take in the world with a gesture — must
amount to something somewhere, mustn't it?
So maybe after unaccountable delays
there'll be a certificate issued, or why not
a trophy whose miniature golfer
chips on to a silver-plate green? Or even

a visiting Belgian milkman weeping
silver tears on the Town Hall steps, outflanked
by weeping coppers, with a chorus of wives.
You may as well wait here until or unless
the parkie moves you on, or you turn up
a hundred-franc note in your sock. Success!

Dear friend, dear maladroit, dear long lost fool,
I watch, since there is nothing I can do.
I watch the smoke uncoiling from your mouth,
and you in turn become the smoke, as though
transcending all the mess there ever was
and rising, slightly, in the freezing air.

# Second Language

You haunt the corridors and offices
of empty premises with yellow calendars
and desk-drawers choked with dust:
beloved labyrinths, archives of pain
from disused objects – inkwells, blotters,
ledgers lying open under sightless clocks
with faces on the brink of revelation.
In these chambers where the future
came and went and left no comment
when the nineteenth century, the erstwhile
capital of everything, was sentenced
to internal exile, you've been listening
at the walls, a spy for history. Some nights
you half-believe you've heard what can't be said.
Which might be agony. Or prayer, perhaps –
a rosary, recited by a relegated god
immured within a ruined paradigm,
or just the banter of some *fonctionnaires*
returning late from lunch, untroubled
by this waiting telegram from death.
Call it a lifetime's work. Time's up.
Snuff out the lamps and leave. If history's
its own reward, you too must be
its language, secret and unspeakable,
forever dying in the act of being born.

## À la Carte

You watch me with companionable coolness.
If at one time we were there or thereabouts,
we lacked the nerve to consummate the illness,
or were preserved by civilizing doubts –
and there the story ends without beginning,
me saying nothing and you not replying.

You might think privately that I go on
too much about this stuff. You might be right.
But in the interval between the last one gone
and who goes next, it gets me through the night,
remembering the hims and hers time once
declared immortal. Time was lying.

*Embrace futurity*, you say. I see
the dark street on the far side of the glass
where we grew up. The waiter glides phantasmally
away, then makes a second pass
when you produce that bottle from your bag –
deadpan as always, as always beguiling.

*But we can't just give in to it*, you say,
and I agree, whatever I might think,
in case you change your mind and put away
the evening's final offer of a drink.
Christ, if the dead could only see us now,
they'd laugh so hard we'd hear them crying.

Theirs are names I still hear in my sleep.
These are the streets. Tonight's the night.
They issued promises they could not keep
to those who could not share their appetite.
They injured those they only wished to honour.
The whole damn thing became too bloody tiring.

Sex and drugs and education
did for some, and cancer claimed the rest;
we spent infinities in lamplit preparation,
but no one ever learned who passed the test,
or whether it was even worth applying.
Meanwhile those of us not busy being dead
re-read the menu carefully. *At least we're trying.*

# Siberian Birch

The snow-pale Siberian birch
is almost bare today, but it goes on
dispensing the host in old-gold wafers
to the poor in spirit who stand
inside us watching in the kitchen
for the end of days, though now
when there have been so many days
this one must surely be forever.

Time is awake, the great insomniac,
and we are time, eaten and eating
as time eats, high up where the numbers
tick softly away and away
along the corridors whose holy books
are sleeping on the matter. You and I
my darling and you my black dog
can always be found in the index.

When we have forgotten our names
and each other, the kiss you give me now
will outlive us. And here we are,
still in the kitchen, still watching the clock —
and whether to be archived in this way
confers on us a consolation
for the rest of it, I have on good authority
we won't be asking when we're done.

# Desire

Time once more to catalogue
the little repertoire of loss
and what preceded it, the white room
emptied and the bare bulb
hanging in the dark. My work is over
thinks desire, then plays the reel

again, to prove that it will only
change by fading, though the appetite
remains, the futile specificity,
the 'rags of time' in the narrow light
of self-regard, the inescapable
conclusion out of which

the new demands are issuing.
Desire will make its own arrangements.
If only for a moment, it must reach
accommodation somewhere,
folding and folding a threadbare towel
at a window looking down

on to a viaduct where wet red lights
watch evening come in blue,
as though it will be different this time
to recognize desire as solitude
and solitude as memory, a skylight
rain a lifetime past is falling on.

# The Goodbye Look

It is never enough. You have to go back
for additional heartbreak and evil,
as if desire could be satisfied by habit.
After all, the past is what you're after:
'the past', that in the dream pretends
an innocent complicity, like Heurtebise
who waits to go with you into the dark.
The mirrored passageways attend you,
staffed with ancient long-case clocks,
their eyebrows arched discreetly.
You again, Monsieur. You never learn.
There is no key, Monsieur, that can unlock
the sepulchre where life and death are one.
You must be satisfied to dream
of curtains blown across the bed
like cloud-rags fleeing from the sky,
with lightning leaping in the mirror.
By what misfortune can you know
so much about a room you'll never enter,
where the object of desire vanishes
the moment that you say her name?
The mansions of the rich are built
to show beyond a shadow of a doubt
that they alone made history, but time's
the evil in the heart of things, the sole
possessor of itself. And time insists:
there was before; there will be after,

no half-measures, nothing in between:
no tarrying here nor flying hence,
and therefore on the night she came
her greeting was the goodbye look
with which she turned away, obedient
to the dark possessor, king of harm,
whose name, as empty and as absolute
as music, is not to be uttered in daylight.
Her greeting was the goodbye look,
a resurrection and a death, a death.
What is it that you cannot understand?

# To Cythera

I live for dying afternoons like this,
to dream of sailing half a century ago
by tea-tray through the pillars of the hearth
with contraband and Rizlas, off
into the sooty night. And you'd remember too,
except you're dead.
                      The ash we leave
is raining on the sea, the ghost of language
only fire can decipher now.
Put on that witchy crimson. Take me there.
You always knew the way to Cythera.

And when I wake, and if I wake,
in Hell, in Hull, in a synopticon of ice
that reeks of smoke and patchouli,
then will time too have ended, ended,
ended like the lives of those I knew
at childhood's end, our age of afternoons,
our autumn, dressed in smoke and rowan-berries,
when your skin was alabaster and the jewel
in the choker you did not remove
deep blue as ocean never was, and yet
I drowned and went on drowning there?

Gone with a smoke-ring, the turn of a page
or a key in a diary, too soon,
as though you could be merely human.
But tonight allow this tinplate quinquereme
to wreck itself on Cythera:
I cannot have it otherwise, no matter
if my selfish sorrow cannot grasp
the dream of you made flesh, implacable
as ever, and the jewel as blue as heaven still.

# Juniper

*in memory of the artist Birtley Aris*

Whatever road we choose will cross
the narrow bridge at Juniper.

A dry bed plunges down the dark
among the alders and the willow-groves.

Where nothing breathes until we're gone
you found a way inside:

now lead us past the gate into temptation
where the facts cannot be told apart

from pen-strokes hatching dark on dark
the silence of the wood at Juniper

that will outlive us
with a movement in the corner of the eye,

black water gliding out of sight
to Juniper, to Juniper.

## This is Not a River

Half of England drains into this water,
but you tell me this is not a river,
yet out of the *strange Midland distances*
*the Trent comes gliding* to be wedded to the Ouse,
while Nidd and Ure and Wharfe and Calder, Aire and Don
have travelled here also, under an alias,
under the cover of night, to gather
at high noon with the Sunne in Splendour
at the turning of the tide, when the sky unfurls
a cloud-assembly robed in white-gold samite
like a company of heralds who will never play
their promised fanfare, because all this water
listens for one song alone in tribute to itself.

Waiting for a train at Goole or Selby
even you, you mere geographer, must sense
the tributaries entering the greater tide,
dispersing in its continental breadth
as if they have arrived, though here is all departure,
sliding and quickening, standing for a moment
on a shingle foreshore, then out beneath the bridge
and past the ruined city which no longer has a say
in how this water runs or where it ends. And yet
you tell me this is not a river. Call it what you like.

The pilings of the jetties are the colour of the mud
they rise from and sink in. So too the head of the poet
that rocks in their shadow, still singing
*Humber, Hebrus, Rhodope and Little Switzerland.*
The beloved was drowned, succumbed to a snakebite,
drank the evil physic proffered by a charlatan
to send her mad. Whatever is the case, it lies
beyond dispute: the poet and his dead bride
and his head walk out together now
among the fields of amaranth where the Wharfe
meanders through Marvell's annihilated Paradise,
or sometimes by the Haven down at Hessle.

*It is said.* The voice is passive and the throat an O
through which the word emerges from no place
to guarantee that on a sofa dumped along the tideline
the lovers and the head may sit to take their rest
on the far shore *where no men abide,*
and that the bloodstained rose the poet offers
to his sleeping love is from the East,
the darkening East, for which this water
you insist is not a river hastens on.

# Fingerpost

*i.m. Paul Harrison*

That fingerpost, illegible. A narrow road
that slips away downhill into the sun,
the faintest implication of a road,
deep in cow parsley, downhill
past shadow-crowded coppices
and yawning gates adorned
with faded admonitions, a road that runs
under the railway and under the river
and finally into the west.
                              Remember that?
We shan't be going now. We'll never find
another time to save it for.
But the road still runs, as well you knew,
down between great copper beeches
and the steep fields after harvest, baked
to the ochre of shortbread,
not forgetting birdsong,
the descant of the rising lark
that never ends, composed of silence.

# The Point

> *part, still, of the done war*
> Thom Gunn, 'Adolescence'

We walked the length of it, the whole great curve
of mud and marram, down the railway track
that served the guns, on past the pilots' cottages
where women wrangled bedsheets in the wind,
into the fort become forest and finally out
to watch the estuary become the sea.
We'd talked of it for years, strategically,
and when at last we managed to arrive
as men of fifty-odd with time to kill,
we stood there at a loss in our success.
It takes you back, we said, the airfield gone,
the sunk emplacements stripped of guns.
Were we still awaiting orders? If we hoped
for some illumination, we were not
so foolish as to think ourselves entitled,
though as the Colonel might have said,
at least we secured the objective.

His war was present to him always.
On the pitch at Spion Kop or at Majuba,
his khaki shorts were likely those he wore
in summer in an Oflag in Silesia.
*Harry them in the loose*, he urged. And if they came
today, the tilted blockhouses were waiting.

So were we. We had the expertise:
conscripts of a teleology
with God's initials, countersigned by Churchill,
we were history. Our nights were spent
in the evil light of a parachute flare
descending on the docks. We had no stories
of our own: we made do in the ruins,
astray among arcades of buddleia
while mad-eyed tramps in British Army Warms
lit fires and drank themselves away.

When National Service ended, we were seven
and the done war was not done with us.
Majuba. Spion Kop. *Remember, men,*
the Colonel said into the cloud of steam
we crouched in at half-time: *harry them
in the loose and in the maul and in the hurly-burly*,
for the honour of the House we understood
was England. The decent Colonel's other loves
were Addison and Steele and Hakluyt, but
I would not join his Corps. Non serviam,
while you were loyal, parading after school
in a cap and webbing. The drill was overseen
by Sergeant Renny, who had walked, he said,
the length of India in this one pair of boots
and then walked home to put you jokers straight.

In all that play-acting with three blank rounds
at Strensall Camp, there lived some gallows joke
whose explanation would be sacrilege.

You were not meant to ask, and so I didn't.
The solitary Mick with no home team,
I mucked in with the rest of it, and learned
to share a balanced and demented admiration
for Bouncing Bombs and Rommel equally.
This was an English study, clothed in fiction
for a borrowed birthright. I revised
by skipping games on Wednesday afternoon
to watch *The Guns of Navarone*, *The Desert Fox*,
*The Great Escape*, *The One That Got Away*,
until my Englishness would pass. And you sat in,
still meaning every word.

                    Then when we came of age,
there were no Messerschmitts for you to fight.
We sent each other histories of combat,
common ground where death rose through the page
at Passchendaele and Ypres and Langemark.
We made our visit to the Point, and then
when we were nearly old, we studied Mametz Wood
from the entrenchment that the Devonshires still hold.
The summer waited on the fields
and in the shadows of the trees, a longing
without name or issue, and I understood
that in the fellowship of slaughter
you had found what you were looking for: a faith,
a chance to share the common fate, to see
the house struck down, if that was what it took.
Flame-capped Achilles stood between us then,
He on whom the gods bestowed the gift of death.

They say that bells can still be heard out here
where the usurper Bolingbroke once knelt
to kiss the salty stones of England's moat,
though as our grandmothers would say: *stop that,
you'll catch your death or summat worse.*
These days the spit's too often breached to walk.
It's almost over, surely as the bungalows
along the red clay coast go over
every day into the longshore drift,
as surely as this fort will be an island
that the sea will claim and drown, as surely
as I look back from the water's edge
to say these things to you, not knowing
where to turn, and find you gone, my friend.

# NOTES

Epigraph: '*After Hölderlin*': This is freely adapted from Hölderlin's 'Hälfte des Lebens'.

'*The Bonfire Party*': Eric Ravilious painted this watercolour on 5 November 1933, having watched the fireworks near his home in Kensington. On 12 November an election was held in Germany following the passage of an act banning all political parties other than the NSDAP. While over three million spoiled ballots were submitted, the Nazis claimed 92% of the vote.

'*Impasse*': I'd read some of Georges Simenon's Maigret novels over the years, but during the Covid pandemic I found myself reading a good many more – not in chronological order, but as I happened upon them in the Penguin series of new translations. I have yet to read them all. I felt the pull of chronology, but I resisted it in favour of entering Maigret's world randomly – an experience analogous to dream-life, where certain motifs (cities, railway stations, libraries, in my case) recur without ever quite abolishing the mystery that animates them. The idea that Simenon is a poet of the crime novel is always somewhere in the offing. I'm sceptical about this. Does he need such an accolade? The term 'poet' seems to be summoned to indicate approval of a rather imprecise kind. On the other hand, economy, precision, selection of significant detail and a sense of inevitable authority in the language itself are among the factors which warrant the comparison. They amount to a vision.

When I began to write the poems, I don't think I had it mind to write a series (still less a sequence). I wanted to identify something in the Simenon *paysage* which nagged at and haunted me, beginning with a canal in the coalfields near the Belgian border, and moving on to a bar in what Auden called 'a decaying port' on the Channel coast. In both cases something has finished but is not over. Belatedness seems endemic in the Maigret world: the past has escaped its occupants in order to imprison them.

Simenon is the only author whose work I've wanted to write about like this, and I allowed myself a reverie on his turf. Whether the result has any illumination to offer I don't know, but I hope the poems give pleasure while honouring a great original.

*'This is not a River'*: 'strange Midland distances' is quoted from Frank Redpath's poem 'Humber (2)', *How It Turned Out: Selected Poems of Frank Redpath*, edited by John Wakeman, The Rialto, Norwich, 1996, p. 31.

'Trent comes gliding' is adapted from W. H. Auden and Christopher Isherwood, *The Dog Beneath the Skin*, Auden, *Plays and Other Dramatic Writings*, edited by Edward Mendelson, Faber, 1989, p. 191.

# ACKNOWLEDGEMENTS

*Aftershock Review, ANAM, Bad Lilies, The Dark Horse, The High Window, One Hand Clapping, Poetry London, PN Review, The Poetry Review, Poetry Salzburg Review, Poetry Scotland, The Process of Poetry, The Robert Graves Review, Stand, The Irish Times, Times Literary Supplement.*

A number of the poems in this collection were included in the chapbook *Impasse: for Jules Maigret*, published by Hercules Editions (2023). Other poems appeared in the pamphlets *Otherwise* (2023) and *Juniper* (2024) from Dare-Gale Press, and *À la Carte* (New Walk, 2025). Thanks are due to the editors.